THE MYTH OF THE TAROT

ABOUT THE AUTHOR

Born in England in 1959, Lance Kelly was introduced to Tarot cards at the age of 12. Fascinated by the mythic symbols, but not yet aware of their true meaning, he ventured out as a young man to embrace the world in the endeavour to fulfil his youthful dreams.

Following a spiritual realisation in 1992 his life completely changed. Soon after this came the teaching of a spiritual master and the love of a woman, both of which had a profound effect on his life. With the reappearance of the Tarot cards came the realisation of the idea behind the Tarot; and it is the practical application of this knowledge that he demonstrates in his Tarot work around the world.

THE MYTH OF THE TAROT

THE AMAZING JOURNEY OF THE FOOL

Lance Kelly

Edited by Marilyn Eve

DRACO PUBLISHING

Edited by Marilyn Eve

Illustrations (and front cover picture of The Fool) from the Tarot De Marseilles
reproduced with kind permission of Wiener Spielkartenfabrik,
Ferd Piatnik and Sons, Vienna. © Piatnik Vienna

Published by Draco Publishing
40 Charles Street. London SW13 0NZ, England

Printed and bound in England by
Titus Wilson and Son, Kendal, Cumbria

ISBN 0 9535521 0 1

CONTENTS

INTRODUCTION

Behind the Tarot is an idea, a power that has been influencing man and shaping his destiny since the dawning of time. Since his earliest beginnings, the impulse within him has been to replicate his own inner nature in form. The images of his earthly existence that he carved and painted as an outward expression of his art were sacred to him as symbols of the formless life within. In time, when human nature began to impose itself as a conflicting force on the natural order of creation, man's connection with his inner reality began to diminish. The simplicity of the primitive spirit gave way to his increasing intellectualism and the need for more complex models to demonstrate his understanding of life and the universe. The Tarot is such a model.

When western civilisation began to flourish, the gnosis – the original knowledge of man – began to filter through to the great body of learning in the West. The western mind, starved since before the Dark Ages of any real knowledge, seized upon the ideas of the East, but distorted their truth through mystification and the love of the occult. This was the endeavour to discover the meaning of life through the pursuit of knowledge, which contributed to a burgeoning of scientific investigation and artistic expression, as well as advancement in more unorthodox practices such as alchemy and astrology.

The Tarot cards evolved through the necessity to preserve, in the language of universal symbolism, a set of instructions to guide man back to his original freedom. The cards appeared for the first time, in a version that would be recognisable today, in fourteenth century Europe. Their fundamental message that personal salvation could be realised through the power of the individual man or woman was in direct conflict with the established papal authority of the day. However, despite the

1

many attempts to abolish the Tarot since it first appeared, it has survived as a remarkable testimony to man's creative spirit.

But what is the purpose of Tarot today? How can a set of ancient symbols, and images of strangely bedecked characters from centuries ago, have any significance in this age of super-technology, through which a constant deluge of information, news and entertainment is transmitted globally? The Tarot's enduring appeal lies in the power of the symbols and the accessibility of the cards themselves. When a rapport with the symbols has been established, the cards act as a mirror, reflecting facets of the psyche that are usually hidden from everyday awareness. This enables those who are sensitive to the inner life to have insights and intimations of the future, for which the Tarot is primarily known. Yet this is only part of it.

The Tarot system is an invention of the mind, a concept of the original idea. The symbols combine to produce a working model, a formal representation of the creative idea itself. There are 78 cards in the Tarot deck, 56 of which are known as the Minor Arcana and, divided into four suits, form the basis of today's playing cards. This book is concerned with the fifth suit – the 22 cards known as the Major Arcana. They tell a story of a character called the Fool and his mythic journey of discovery, with nothing but his love of the unknown to support him. There are three parts to each symbol: the mythic story, a commentary examining the symbolism, and a general guide for divinatory readings.

Myth is the romance of life, the essence of virtue and nobility through which the spirit of mankind can impart its eternal truth. Man and woman are the principal players, whose irresistible attraction to each other is the basis for all the great myths of antiquity. Yet, is myth to be confined to the heroic deeds of those immortalised through fable and legend? Or could it be that the mythic quality of love, chivalry and valour is the true character of the individual, underneath the doubts and fears that obscure the passion for life?

The power of myth has to be demonstrable if it is to have any reality; for the truth is what is lived, whether in the garden, in the office, or at the kitchen sink. Love, wherever it appears, is the bridge to the mythic world, yet the way is often blocked by compromise and familiarity in everyday living. The challenge to bring myth alive is in life itself, mirrored in woman's deep yearning to be loved and man's longing to be worthy of her love — to be the hero he truly knows himself to be.

How this is accomplished is revealed in the myth of the Tarot and the amazing journey of the Fool.

Lance Kelly

Into ignorance you must descend, Child of the Earth,
To do what you must do.
Though in your innocence you leave me, as you must,
To tread the well-worn path of lust,
Take heart, for the world exists to teach you
That all you seek as gain
Can never be life's true delight
And is sure to cause you pain.

So go now, Fool! Though hear me well
And serve your time in living hell.
Be consumed by the world's delights;
Travel far into the western night.
When it's time, and not before,
I shall knock upon your door.
Will you hear me? Would it matter?
Above the din of idle chatter?

What will you do? This is your life.
Can there be freedom without sacrifice?

THE FOOL

The Myth of the Fool

The natural state of the Fool was joy: as the Child of the Earth, it was his birthright. The glorious creation was the reflection of his own inner nature, harmoniously attuned to all his needs. But the love and simplicity in his body was to gradually recede, for there was a stirring within him that was beginning to gather time.

The Fool could resist no longer the subtle excitation that moved him to look beyond the walls of the Garden. Oblivious to the pleas of the mother love, he set out for the experience that he craved. The strange new energy that tantalised him had disturbed the peace of life on earth for evermore.

Unaware of the challenges that lay ahead, the Fool ventured further into the unknown. As the gentle resonance of love within him diminished, the first rush of fear rippled through his body. Reaching out to the rising emotion, he attached himself to the cord of existence; and for the first time he knew wanting.

The Fool was now in a process beyond his control. Suddenly he was accelerating through a passage towards a shaft of light. Carried on a wave of swelling inner pressure, he was thrust through a porthole and landed with a jolt on the other side. He had passed through the ring of forgetfulness onto the surface of existence.

As the Fool came into his senses he saw discord in his strange new surroundings. Menacing shadows appeared to take on form through the haze of his confusion, and even nature was solidifying around him in this alien world where everything was separate from him.

The Fool sought the reassuring nourishment of the earth within his body. But something very precious had gone, for he could no longer withdraw at will into the natural joy of life. Stranded in existence, he was now compelled to find that which he had lost.

The journey into ignorance had begun.

LE·MAT·

THE FOOL / LE MAT

SYMBOLISM

The Fool is the innocence that loves from the innermost being and responds to life with a spontaneity that is not obscured by the emotional shadow of doubt. Through the process of living, everyone makes a unique contribution to life on earth. As the Fool travels through the Tarot, so do I, the individual man or woman, journey through existence in an endeavour to discover something that is real and enduring.

In the Tarot card, the Fool is pictured in travellers' clothes. On his back he carries a sack; inside it is the life that awaits him, the future experience that must be lived out to realise his true potential. Leaving behind the comfort and security of his homeland, he is inspired to find something of value to serve and is prepared, should it be necessary, to die for it. Clinging to his leg is a creature, symbolising all that would hold him back. With no number to pin him down, the Fool has the freedom to transcend any limitations of the past, given sufficient will and sense of purpose. His staff connects him to the earth, keeping him straight and true in facing his life in whatever form it takes.

As the Fool journeys through space and time, the echo of eternity reverberates within him. This is the impulse of life that compels man to discover his original freedom. When distanced from the known, he sees every moment afresh in the letting go of the old. The reverse happens when creative expression is stifled and he feels trapped in the compromise of living, unable to break free from the umbilical cord that binds him to the past.

The Fool is the eternal optimist and shrugs off any mishap or inconvenience that comes his way. Supremely adaptive to the natural environment, he delights in the glorious earth as a child in his playground. Yet his innocence cannot save him from the corruption of the world, for without the necessary experience to walk through it unscathed he is vulnerable to manipulation. So, ultimately, he must venture out: to be responsible for his life in the realisation of his true destiny. This is reflected in the story of the Tarot, in which each encounter serves to contribute towards his life's purpose. When sufficiently seasoned through the trials of existence, the Fool is ready to begin the epic journey home – the inner descent back through the human psyche to the source of his own sweet nature.

DIVINING THE FOOL

The Fool is the key to the Tarot in that he is the means to unlocking the mysteries of the pack. His courage may be unrecognised by others, for the deeds of one who dares to stand alone will always be questioned by those who are left behind.

As an OPENING card, the Fool symbolises the opportunity for action. His character is such that he may pick up his sack at a moment's notice with an eagerness to undertake any new adventure which presents itself. It is therefore advisable that he makes adequate provision for the journey.

As a card in ASSISTANCE, the Fool can indicate that it is now time to take a chance. He reveals that the necessary inspiration is present to embark on a new challenge. There is also a readiness to receive instruction and a willingness to be guided.

In OPPOSITION, the Fool's innocence and spontaneity may lead him to action for which he is inadequately prepared, through lack of experience in the world. The practicality of a situation should be reviewed or further advice sought before undertaking a venture.

As the OUTCOME of an enquiry, the Fool can symbolise the resolve to be true. This may mean the end of a compromise and a time to move on, regardless of ridicule or criticism. There is great potential for change, as long as the questioner does not look back.

❄

THE MAGICIAN

The Myth of the Magician

The Fool had entered existence and was now a prisoner in time. In abandoning the timeless place of his origins, he had set in motion the idea of a world that he could build with his own genius and creativity.

The moments when he could rest content within his natural state of well-being were slowly disappearing. The strange energy that had entered him now seemed to be invading his entire body. This alien and destructive presence was the Magician.

The Fool, unable to resist the seductive enticement of the invader, was soon possessed. The further he travelled, the more he became accustomed to the Magician's changing feelings and began to enjoy the illusions that coloured his perception of life. Sometimes the thoughts that flickered across his mind would be elevating; at other times they would drag him into gloom.

As the Fool became entrenched in the Magician's habit, there emerged a devilish streak to his nature that would erupt without warning. In the company of other Magicians, a confrontation of opposing forces would often ensue. From these encounters he saw that the weaknesses of his fellows could be exploited, using cunning and deception to outwit them for power and prestige.

The natural joy and delight that had been the Fool's birthright had all but disappeared. Now an individual identity separated from the whole, he had become a creator in his own right, a Magician capable of trickery and illusion. In making the leap through the porthole of time, the Fool was now responsible for his world. As the Magician, he was yet unaware of his true purpose in life, for only the living process itself would reveal, in time, what had to be done.

The Fool melded into existence. When the Magician's box of tricks had been exposed, he would be ready to move on.

I

LE BATELEUR

I

THE MAGICIAN / LE BATELEUR

SYMBOLISM

The Magician is man. In his finest moments he is the creative spirit itself: in his darkest, he is the devil. His power to work magic for the good of all has deteriorated in time. An inevitable build-up of force has now led to conflict and fear, disturbing the simplicity of his inner state of love. Through his worship of materialism and progress, he has developed the means of his own destruction and brought himself, and the world, to the brink of annihilation.

The various items on the Magician's table are the contents of the Fool's sack. The cups, coins, blades and the wand held in the Magician's hand are the fragments of his divided self; collectively they make up the materials of his life's potential that will influence, and be influenced by, the forces of creation. As the Magician has created his world with his box of tricks, so must he toil in it. Transfixed by his magical prowess and unable to handle the consequences of his actions, he is rarely fulfilled by the limited power of creativity now available to him. Addicted to experience, both the good and the bad, he dissipates his creative energies in innumerable distractions. Only when he has immersed himself in the uncertainty of living for sufficient time can there be the possibility that he may awake from his dream.

The Magician's true purpose is to be sovereign of the earth: to utilise his creative genius in loving union with woman, his mate. In his betrayal and desertion of her throughout the ages, he has abandoned the source of his creativity and now looks to the world for his pleasure. Dressed in his finery, he is the strutting cockerel who displays his wares to an adoring audience. Obsessed with his own self-image, he is unable to face the awful truth of his avoidance of love and looks away, engrossed in his own games-playing.

The restless Magician, now no longer able to retain the presence of his divine state of being, has introduced to woman through physical love the excitement and momentum of his pent-up negative energies. Increasingly alienated from her feminine passivity, she now doubts her love and replicates his projective thrust in her endeavour to compete in his world.

However, the impulse within every Magician is to create with the materials on his table the finest expression of his love. He forever seeks that sacred place of his beloved where, in union, he may realise the source of his true magicianship. Somehow he must be turned inside out to be made worthy of entering the shrine, the domain of the High Priestess.

DIVINING THE MAGICIAN

The Magician symbolises the creative essence itself. He is the supreme artist, whose life's work is measured by his power to love.

As an OPENING card, the Magician is poised with his box of tricks to work his magic. He can symbolise a need for artistic expression and the yearning for acknowledgement and love. He can sometimes represent someone of great influence in the questioner's life.

As a card in ASSISTANCE, the Magician is in a powerful placement with all the necessary materials available to be creative. He can symbolise the ability to communicate with flair and versatility.

In OPPOSITION, he can be evasive and able to manipulate a situation with a masterful sleight of hand. To know him requires self-knowledge, for he is not what he appears to be. This is especially relevant in relationships, where emotive issues can highlight the Magician's avoidance of love.

As the OUTCOME of an enquiry, the Magician, brimming with confidence and enthusiasm, can symbolise an unlimited potential for creative expression. Since he is prone to self-deception, however, he must take care not to lose touch with the source of his original inspiration.

❄

THE HIGH PRIESTESS

The Myth of the High Priestess

The Magician could no longer hold his world together. His creative genius had run amok. Looking at the chaos and suffering he had inflicted upon the earth, he sank to his knees in despair. Never had he felt so wretched and alone. He had been split open, with the two parts of himself locked in a battle for the possession of his body. One half compelled him to move on, whilst the other implored him to go back to the illusory world he had created.

As the conflicting forces raged within, he sensed in the space between them a strangely familiar presence. She appeared from behind a veil, untarnished by the world in her transcendent beauty and mystery. She was the High Priestess, the shrine of love on earth. In her hands was a book of great antiquity: it was the story of the Fool. As she read, the Magician listened, utterly absorbed as the knowledge of his forgotten origins was re-awakened. She revealed how his love of the world had crystallised in time into an unhappy self, an entity whose presence had corrupted the natural innocence of the Fool.

The High Priestess was his eternal opposite, the beloved whom he had deserted to build his world. She was within every woman on earth behind the veil of doubts and fears that had enshrouded her love. His task was to find her in existence: to dissolve the time in himself that divided him from his love. He would have to be purged of his selfish desires, for only in the purity of love could she be reached. Love itself would be his teacher.

As the High Priestess withdrew, the Magician became aware of a font of power arising within him. It was his own inner knowledge, the awakening of the truth of himself. No longer concerned by his box of tricks, he tore at his costume until it resembled that of a humble traveller. Stepping into the unknown, he was a Fool once more.

II

LA PAPESSE

II

THE HIGH PRIESTESS / LA PAPESSE

SYMBOLISM

The High Priestess, in her serenity and grace, is the indefinable beauty within every woman on earth. So subtle and fine is her essence that, in the progressive world of the Magician, she does not exist. The source of her power emanates from her womb, the domain of love inside every woman. From this sacred place, intimations of the inner world communicate a profound knowledge that transcends the physical realm.

Her presence is intuited in the innocent yearning for love. In the Tarot card, she sits with her open book at the entrance to her shrine. She spends her time absorbed by the stories that delighted her as a child, of the heroic deeds of her knight who somehow overcame any challenge to be united with her, his beloved. Today she can no longer be reached so easily, for the romantic dreams of youth are soon punctured by the harsh reality of existence. The emotional traumas that accompanied her experience of romance have engendered fear and distrust, restricting her natural inclination to give herself totally in the intimacy of love. Now protected by an almost impenetrable barrier of past hurts and disappointments, she is reluctant to open herself again to man. Starved of love, and manipulated through excitement and fear, she doubts herself; and in her confusion and despair may give up on him altogether.

Thus did the High Priestess withdraw into her inner sanctum where she now waits to be reached, protected from the duplicity of the world. It is in her passivity that she retains her power, for this is the mystery in woman that man adores. She is his missing part, the feminine side of his nature. His eternal quest (and the impulse behind all his artistic and worldly pursuits) is to be worthy to enter her shrine. His only impediment is his fear to truly love, for within him is the knowledge that to reach her he must sacrifice his most treasured possession – his substitute love of the world. This is the hardest thing on earth to do, for the world is the mirror of his self.

The Fool has cast off the Magician's habit. He must now begin to dismantle the negativity that separates him from his love. Only in his humility and noble purpose can he contain her transcendent beauty through the gradual realisation of the one divine woman, the essence of the High Priestess.

DIVINING THE HIGH PRIESTESS

The High Priestess is the font of inner knowledge, imparting her wisdom through the purity of love. Sometimes elusive, she may require a subtlety of perception to divine her ethereal essence.

As an OPENING card, the High Priestess is endeavouring to reveal a hidden quality to enable the questioner to see something with greater clarity. The current situation may offer the opportunity to bring to the surface an emotional disturbance from the past to be examined in the light of present knowledge.

As a card in ASSISTANCE, the High Priestess symbolises a highly receptive state and an intuitive knowledge relating to the nature of the enquiry. There is the potential to bring into existence something of great value to the questioner's life.

In OPPOSITION, the subtle intimations of the High Priestess can be easily distorted. Hidden anxieties in the form of self-doubt and fear may be obscuring the questioner's clarity. These may have been formed through the traumas of childhood and the absorption of emotional conflict. There may now be a need be more open to life and love.

As the OUTCOME of an enquiry, the High Priestess communicates the need to follow one's own intuitive knowledge. This may often go against the feelings and advice of others, but in overcoming any fear or hesitation in doing what is known to be right, there can be a new confidence in one's own ability.

❄

THE EMPRESS

THE MYTH OF THE EMPRESS

The Fool, awakened by the High Priestess to the subtle resonance of his inner knowledge, had continued his journey. There in a beautiful garden he saw her, the outer reflection of his formless love within. In her serenity she reflected the harmony of nature, and the sweet fragrance of life resonated in her flesh as living love. She was the Empress, the essence of Mother Earth. In her garden everything was provided, eternally replenished by the cycle of the seasons.

She said that she was going to introduce him to love, to reveal the true purpose of his quest. The Empress had been loved divinely. One day as she sat alone in the forest, a man had appeared. She had recognised him at once, for he had come to restore her to the earth. He had declared that he would love her with noble purpose until she was united for ever with the source of her own true nature. Willing to sacrifice all that she had known, she had surrendered completely to love.

She was now the eternal mother in the vastness of her being. Like a magnet, she had attracted the Fool to instruct him in the ways of love. In the coming together in the flesh, her wisdom could be imparted in the fullness of her sensual beauty.

It was a painful and disorientating time for the Fool as the impersonal love of the Empress ruthlessly penetrated the resistance of his self. In the purifying of his body, he was gradually able to receive her divine energies, and the seed of love was sown.

When it was time to leave, the Empress returned to her garden. The Fool, with the essence of her precious gift within him, was now ready to face whatever he might have to encounter to bring this love into the world.

III

L'IMPERATRICE

III

THE EMPRESS / L'IMPERATRICE

SYMBOLISM

The Empress is woman, the sensual expression of love in existence. As the High Priestess symbolises the inner reality of the feminine principle, so the Empress embodies her transcendent beauty in form. Receptive to her environment, she reflects her inner state of love, giving where she can in the sweetness and abundance of her nature.

In the Tarot card, the Empress is seated on her throne, protected by the artefacts of state. The sceptre bestows upon her the sovereignty of her earthly domain. Her shield deflects the forces of the world and absorbs the pain of existence. The eagle emblazoned on her shield symbolises her power to awaken man, when he is ready, to the knowledge of his noble purpose. She waits passively in her resolve to be true to love, her wings symbolising the power latent within every woman to reach this place of purity. It is her delight to be with man of love, but she knows that in his present condition he is not yet himself.

The Empress is the serene beauty of woman, the irresistible magnet for man. Sensing her unattainable mystery in the reflection of the glorious earth, he climbs the highest mountains to be embraced by the impersonal nature of her love. Yet whatever he achieves, he can never be fulfilled for long. His quest to conquer himself in the world is the search for his missing part. This is woman, who waits for him to come to her in love.

In man's betrayal of the Empress, he has engendered in her a fearsome loathing which arises to assail him as the reflection of his own failure to love. She who has absorbed the tyranny and heartbreak throughout the ages is now, like the plundered earth, a shadow of her former glory. Her power to radiate the purest expression of love is often distorted by the turgidity of intense negative emotions. Frequently seduced by the lure of the world, she lays down her shield and sceptre in the abdication of her command of love.

However, this does not change her reality, for in her maturity the Empress can undergo a transformation. Experienced in love and knowledgeable of life, she can release much of the burden she has carried. Transcending her personal love, she then encompasses the

27

whole, with both inner and outer hemispheres aligned, as the personification of Mother Earth.

DIVINING THE EMPRESS

Wherever she appears, the Empress will grace a reading with her stabilising presence. She has a great capacity to endure extraordinary hardship, forever giving of herself as long as there is love and a sense of purpose.

As an OPENING card, the Empress can symbolise a selfless and practical approach in assessing the needs of the situation. There can be a longing to provide a nurturing environment, perhaps to replicate the intimacy of the mother love.

As a card in ASSISTANCE, the Empress, in a state of poise and equanimity, indicates harmony in her surroundings. The questioner may proceed with confidence in the knowledge that there is nourishment and support in abundance.

In OPPOSITION, the Empress questions the purpose of one's actions. There may be other matters that have to be resolved before sufficient ground can be established to move on. This placement can reflect disharmony in one's surroundings due to the lack of acknowledgement and support from others, often in a family situation.

As the OUTCOME, the Empress is a magnet, attracting through the presence of love whatever is necessary for the harmonious solution to the enquiry. There is the potential for the questioner's finest qualities to be revealed, and a sense of fulfilment in the reflection of one's love in existence.

❄

THE EMPEROR

THE MYTH OF THE EMPEROR

The Emperor's word was law. He ruled without compromise. His sense of justice and truth emanated from his being; in this he was utterly incorruptible.

The Fool was to be instructed in the qualities of discipline and command. His initial duties were gruelling. When one task was finished, the Emperor would appear immediately and give him another. Frequently the Fool would collapse with exhaustion. Unable to employ the cunning and tricks of the Magician, he now had to serve his time in recompense to the world for all that he had squandered in the past.

For a long time, the Fool endured his ordeal while the Emperor watched from the wings. Whenever there was a sign of weakness, the Emperor would confront him, ruthless in his endeavour to break the Fool's resistance.

The Emperor embodied the nobility of man. Sometimes he would summon the Fool to accompany him in attending to the affairs of the realm. Bestowed with absolute power, he was courteous to his subjects, acknowledging the purpose and integrity of all things in existence. It was the Fool's challenge to replicate this within himself: to be sovereign of his inner kingdom.

Eventually came the dawning of the Fool's own authority and command. He had undergone an extraordinary transformation. Within his being, he could now perceive the energetic presence of the Emperor as the pristine clarity of the cosmos, encompassing the beauty of the Empress as the glory of the blessed earth. It was he, the Emperor, who had loved her divinely; the Fool, in sharing in this love, was now sacredly connected to him, the noble ruler of man.

With the two hemispheres of creation aligned, the Fool was ready to continue his journey.

IIII

L´EMPEREUR

IIII

THE EMPEROR / L'EMPEREUR

SYMBOLISM

The Emperor symbolises the masculine principle in existence. His influence on civilisation in his endeavour to be an effective ruler of the people is recorded in the history books. However, in his pursuit of power over others instead of himself, the once noble ruler of man forfeited his right to rule. In the abdication of his responsibility for his own inner state, he surrendered his authority; and today he is answerable only to the demands of bureaucracy.

The Emperor's sceptre originally bestowed upon him absolute command, and unquestionable loyalty from his subjects. No longer the symbol of his worthiness to rule, it has become hard and unyielding, represented by his tower blocks and structures of steel. He now rules from a position of rigidity instead of from an openness and justice emanating directly from his place of power within. Unable to combat the pressure of materialism in the progressive world, he has solidified into the concrete of matter and is impossible to budge – except when it suits him. His eagle-crested shield rooted to the earth is a reminder of his potential for transformation.

Although the Emperor's character as the symbol of the true authority in man remains virtually dormant, he is always here. He emerges in times of crisis as a pillar of strength and stability, his courage and resolve invoking loyalty and respect from those around him; in his compassion and loving ways, he is the father and guardian; and he is the protector who offers his practicality and worldly wisdom to guide and assist those in need.

The Emperor is born to be a natural leader. His real kingdom is as vast as the universe, yet his universal vision is obscured by the limitation of his worldly domain. Now identified with his need for financial security above all else, he is unable to soar beyond the pressures of his material existence. In facing himself he has to withstand the forces that keep him emotionally volatile, which he perpetuates by the excitement and delirium of his speculative mind. The hostility, poverty and greed in the world are the outer reflection of what is energetically stored within him. His woman, who is often at the receiving end of his wrath when

33

what he wants is denied him, is the prize he must somehow regain. This is his greatest challenge of all.

DIVINING THE EMPEROR

The Emperor is custom-built for the world. However, it is often at the height of temporal power and success that there is an awakening of a deeper yearning for something beyond the material realm.

As an OPENING card, the Emperor indicates a solid foundation on which to build. This can be a clear signpost to proceed, but there may be a need to maintain a flexible approach, as there can sometimes be a rigidity in dealing with others.

As a card in ASSISTANCE, he symbolises a worldly authority and the ability to take command of a situation. There can be a great resolve and determination to accomplish a task. The Emperor may symbolise a powerful figure, giving his support as benefactor or protector.

In OPPOSITION, he often appears as a figure in authority who may have a hold over the questioner. He can symbolise the influence of the father, who may have displayed a hardness and dogged refusal to listen through his own fear and dishonesty to love. There may now be a need to break with a situation, or to abandon one's own fixed position.

As the OUTCOME of an enquiry, the Emperor is able to consolidate any fragments around him to bring about a practical solution. Disciplined and one-pointed, he can symbolise a successful campaign, often bringing material gain. In some instances, the sacrifice in the attainment of worldly recognition may be too high a price to pay.

❄

THE POPE

The Myth of the Pope

The Fool recognised him at once. He was the ancient one who had been in existence since the dawning of time as custodian of the original knowledge of life.

He was the Master, the personification of the living truth. Attracted by an omniscient power, the Fool had gravitated towards him. It was a great privilege to be in the presence of such a man. Imparting the wisdom of the ages with clarity and simplicity, the Master revealed that the true purpose of existence was to be free of the burden of time.

Listening in wonder, the Fool was enveloped by the stillness of his being as he descended into a place of peace beyond the wavering mind. He perceived in the Master the light of the Lord, and held in love and gratitude that which he had received. In this was the acknowledgement of the truth of life within that had awakened his love of the unknown.

The Fool had opened himself completely to the divine inspiration of the Master, and was now prepared to devote his life to serve him. This was not to be. It was revealed that the Fool's destiny could only be realised in the theatre of the world. The truth he had absorbed would now have to be lived to test his resolve against the forces of creation. Life would be his teacher, but the presence of the Master would always be within him.

Released from the Master's orbit, the Fool continued his journey alone. Isolated from his fellow man, he questioned the purpose of his life. Within him the calling of the High Priestess arose, reminding him of his noble quest to find her in existence. The truth was realised within; but it was in the world that woman, the mirror of his love, awaited him.

V

LE PAPE

V

THE POPE / LE PAPE

SYMBOLISM

The Pope is the true spiritual father. He is partially represented in existence as a teacher, religionist, scientist or academic to fulfil in some way the evolutionary needs of the individual.

In the Tarot card, the Pope is seated in front of two pillars. Since the earliest civilisations, the pillar has been seen as a symbol of great power. Its vertical line represented man's freedom to withdraw at will to unite with his own inner reality. The original pillar, the divine oneness and absolute unity of life, is now split into two, creating a duality in the mind of man. The pillar to the left is the female repository of inner knowledge. This is pure life in a state of unwavering poise, which is beyond the rational mind. The right-hand pillar is the male principle, the means through which the pure potential of life is expressed externally in existence. The triple-tiered cross is the bridge between the physical, psychic and spiritual realms. In accordance with the responsibility taken for life, the Pope is permitted to transverse these realms at will to assist those who are drawn to be with him. The two figures before him symbolise his former ignorance, now appearing outside of him to be raised to his own level of consciousness.

The knowledge of man's origins was once retained as a living state, as a divine presence or consciousness. This was the gnostic idea of the power within the man through which union with God could be realised. At the time of the emerging Christian religion, the founding church fathers effectively banished the God within, necessitating hope and the notion of a future heaven or saviour outside the integrity of the individual. The gnostics, unable to conform to the priestly dogma, disappeared beneath the gathering stampede of western civilisation.

However, the original gnosis has survived; for, finally, the Pope is the symbol of the spiritual Master. He is not a priest, but one who has realised the profundity of his own being. The dawning of the truth, when it is time, can manifest the living Master in the external world. He is recognised by his simplicity and extraordinary presence, which allows the truth to be received direct and not through any distracting medium. The Master is the surrogate father for those who are living his teaching, informing and instructing them of his realisation through the culture and events of his time.

DIVINING THE POPE

The Pope is able to apply the intuitive knowledge of the High Priestess in the external world. He can instruct and advise from a place of great wisdom and experience of life, and can guide the individual to the source of original knowledge.

As an OPENING card, the Pope symbolises the questioner's need for an area of life to be clarified in order to reveal its true meaning. He can indicate a change in direction and, possibly, a yearning to discover the deeper significance of life.

As a card in ASSISTANCE, the Pope can indicate that there is sufficient knowledge available to proceed with a course of action. He can symbolise a teacher, or someone who is influential in the questioner's life. There may be the opportunity to investigate a new area of study.

In OPPOSITION, the Pope questions the wisdom to proceed in the intended direction. More facts may need to be obtained before further commitment. There may also be a need to examine a personal belief system that originates from an authority figure or institution.

As the OUTCOME of an enquiry, the Pope endeavours to raise the consciousness of the individual and to connect him with the source of his own integrity. There can be the realisation that what was sought as a solution outside oneself is already known. There is often a profound insight into a situation through the ability to apply one's knowledge, free from impediment and the limitations of the past.

❄

THE LOVERS

The Myth of the Lovers

She was there as woman at the behest of love. In the first moment he saw her, the waves of love flooded through him, everything fading from his mind save for her beautiful image. Romance and courtship ensued and, in time, the Fool and his beloved were lovers.

The Fool had found his sweetheart. In the beginning they were inseparable in the wonder and beauty of their love. Joyous in the sweetness of his beloved's presence, the Fool was in paradise.

The first sign that love was wavering came without warning. Beginning with a sudden harsh word, a change began to manifest in the Fool's behaviour. An ominous shadow would darken his joy, making him restless and sullen. It was the power of love that was stirring the hidden mass of his unhappy self, which had lain dormant until now.

One day, unable to contain his growing agitation any longer, the Fool demanded that he be given time to be alone. The all-consuming passion of woman was testing his honesty to love, by making him confront the ignorance of his past. She said that she loved him dearly; but if he could no longer be with her in love, then he must go.

The Fool, unable to withstand the pressure of his self, left her to travel to the ends of the earth. Try as he might to lose himself in the world, the image of his beloved would continually besiege him. Separated from his love, he saw that his wilful ways had foiled his noble quest to truly love woman in the surrender of his self. He would return to make amends for his betrayal, for the seed of love was still within him.

It took a long time to demonstrate his earnest intention to face that which he had avoided. The Fool and his sweetheart were reunited as lovers. Through the constant vigilance to preserve the flame of love, their joy and pleasure would frequently transcend the senses in the knowledge of a higher purpose in their sacred union as lovers.

VI

THE LOVERS / L'AMOUREUX

SYMBOLISM

Man is the great lover, yet his creativity is dispersed through his many other loves in the world in the pursuit of power and prestige. His deepest longing is to love with the passion that he senses is within him. In abdicating his true authority as the Emperor, he has substituted the love of woman, the symbol of the earth, with a degenerate love of his self, the symbol of the world.

In the Tarot card, a young man looks bewildered and unsure of which way to turn. His love has split into two. The woman to the right appears in her beautiful form as the mirror of his love. In the woman to the left he sees his own male reflection, the sordid degradation of his love. Hovering above the three figures is Eros, appearing from another realm as a symbol of the power of love which will never let man rest until he heals his divided self.

The essence of the Lovers is love's endeavour to purify man and woman of their unhappiness. This requires that they be true to love and not their fluctuating feelings and emotions. When man is identified with sexual excitement, he is unable to perceive the subtlety and stillness of love through the coarseness of his emotional energy. To enter the body of woman with noble purpose, he must be fearless, for within her is the pain of existence – his own male energy of sex. Only in his selflessness can he reach her, for it requires the ultimate sacrifice: the surrender of his need for self-gratification. This is mostly unacceptable to man as he is, as there is nothing in it for himself but the affirmation from woman that she is truly being loved. However, within him is the knowledge that she is the means to his salvation, for only woman can break him of his substitute love of the world.

Man's greatest fear is losing his independence. It is seen as the last bastion of his freedom, which he steadfastly protects by keeping love at a distance. When woman gets too close to him, he can feel threatened and resort to undermining her in the fear of exposing his own failure to love. Woman, often manipulated by her fear of losing him, relinquishes her power as the Empress; and in giving way to his greater assertiveness, doubts herself in love.

The Fool, in questioning the nature of love, has realised that it is woman, the feminine principle, whom he has always adored. Now that he has seen this, there is no turning back. He must be eroded by love to the state of nothing before love itself can be known. This is the challenge of the Lovers.

DIVINING THE LOVERS

The fluid nature of the Lovers often mirrors, with subtlety and fineness, the essence of love itself, unifying wherever possible the deeply hidden emotions within an individual.

As an OPENING card, the Lovers can symbolise an apparent choice of direction. It can be a turning point in a relationship or situation where hidden emotions may now be surfacing. In the resolve to be more honest in love, there is a great potential to heal deep psychological wounds of the past.

As a card in ASSISTANCE, the Lovers can indicate a profound change in perception within the questioner. In the deepening knowledge of the purpose of love, there is the courage to face oneself and, if necessary, to take action to sever one's ties to a situation that no longer serves.

In OPPOSITION, love is endeavouring to shine through, but there can be a resistance to the new through the holding on to the negativity of past hurts. Indecision and self-doubt may be present, with a reluctance to face the fact. There could be parental or other influence resulting in a pressure to conform to a notion or concept of behaviour.

As an OUTCOME of an enquiry, the Lovers may symbolise a renewal of resources as a result of taking action. It may signal the end of a period of frustration and uncertainty, and a new clarity to perceive the presence of love.

❄

THE CHARIOT

THE MYTH OF THE CHARIOT

In the intimate embrace of love, the Fool looked into his beloved's eyes. As a deepening sense of stillness came upon him, he sank into the blackness of his being. Within him was the knowledge that somewhere in the void, waiting to be reached, was the divine essence of woman.

The Fool had entered a tunnel. At first, the subtlety of love kept him finely balanced in his senses, and his descent was unencumbered. In a moment of self-doubt, when a wave of sheer pleasure threatened to overwhelm him, he was thrown off balance and found himself back at the opening. He descended again, yet the further he travelled, the more difficult it became to retain his equilibrium.

An intense vibration now began to shake his body as the walls of the tunnel reverberated with the energies of his self-indulgent past. These were the emotions of his dishonesty to love, screaming in vehemence at him to go back. Looking straight ahead, he beheld a ring of light at the end of the tunnel; yet it seemed impossible to reach. The Fool despaired. He knew that to enter the sacred shrine of woman he must take nothing for himself. Valiantly he went forth towards her and surrendered himself to love.

All fear and uncertainty now fell away as the Fool realised his noble purpose. At his command was a chariot, with horses aligned in supreme harmony and grace. Majestically contained in the unity of love, he advanced towards the light and passed through the end of the tunnel into a sublime place of beauty.

Returning upwards into his senses, the Fool gently kissed his beloved, the one in whose mystery he had shared. For a magnificent moment he had come of age: the divine Charioteer.

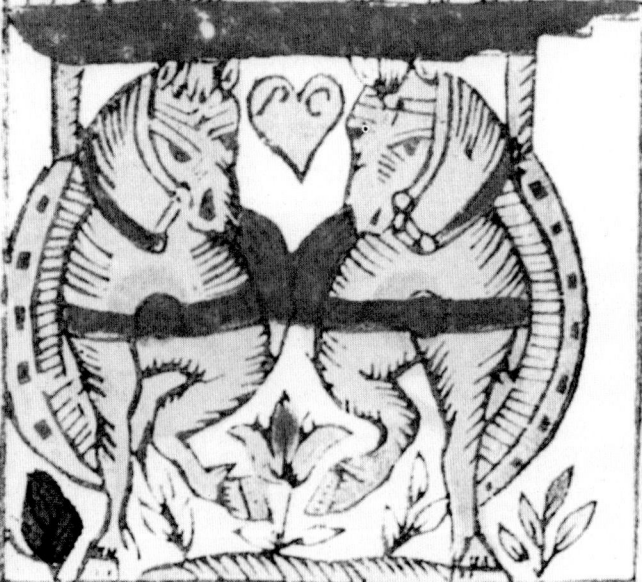

VII

THE CHARIOT / LE CHARIOT

SYMBOLISM

The Fool has shed his sack and travellers' clothes for the robes of state. As the Lovers symbolised the turning point in his journey, so the Chariot embodies his coming of age. With a disciplined team of horses at his command, he is now poised to exceed the limitations of the world. What he will do with his command will be a test of his maturity and worthiness for the greater responsibility of his ultimate destiny. This lies beyond the canopy of the chariot, which, until he is ready, shades him from the full glare of the sun – his own radiant being.

In the Tarot card, the charioteer is seen triumphant on his victory parade. With his vision fixed on the road ahead, he is unconcerned with what lies beyond the boundaries of his worldly domain. The chariot is the vehicle that carries him on his charge through existence; this is the body of his hard-won experience, which allows him to function effectively in the world. The horses symbolise the inner reserves available to fuel his vitality and stamina. In a frenzied, undisciplined condition, they can disrupt the equilibrium of his chariot; but when he is able to harness their energies, the charioteer can rise above the mediocrity of the masses to emerge in a blaze of glory as a prince among men. On his shoulders are his epaulettes, depicting two heads. These signify the severing of personal consideration in his resolve to break with any negative influences that would hinder his progress.

There are two possible directions in which the chariot may travel. One involves the drive into the world, where the charioteer has the ability to generate power and prestige. This outer fixation with materialism consumes, by necessity, most of his energy and the greater part of his life's potential. Eventually he may be moved to dismantle the entire structure to discover the source of his inner reality. This, the journey inwards, is the other direction and is a process of negation.

When turning within, the first thing the charioteer encounters is his own sexual frustration. From this arises the coarse vibration of anger and discontent which makes him unable to remain still for long. In his willingness to confront the turbulence of his unbridled emotions, he is able to refine the raw energy of his charges into the subtle resonance of love. He can then love woman with a greater sensitivity, enabling both chariot and charioteer to harmonise in a unified body of love.

DIVINING THE CHARIOT

The Chariot symbolises the indomitable spirit of man, blazing his trail through existence. When sufficiently focused on an objective, the charioteer is virtually unstoppable in his pursuit of glory.

As an OPENING card, the Chariot is powerfully placed, signifying confidence and the skilful handling of a situation. The questioner is poised to overcome any adversity, but there is a need to contain his energy on the way.

As a card in ASSISTANCE, the Chariot can symbolise the stamina and vigour to carry the questioner through an intense period of activity. There can be a tendency to persevere to the limit of endurance, utilising the full capacity of energy reserves. This may be a temporary measure to enable the completion of a task.

In OPPOSITION, there may be a build-up of pressure through an inability to handle a situation, resulting in a period of turbulence and instability. The charioteer may be travelling in the wrong direction.

As an OUTCOME of an enquiry, the Chariot symbolises success and confirms that everything is set for victory. However, it is imperative for the charioteer to harness his extraordinary energy; otherwise there is the risk of burn-out.

❄

JUSTICE

THE MYTH OF JUSTICE

The flight of the Chariot was over. After soaring to exalted heights, the Fool was now grounded. By his voluntary descent into the profundity of love, he had penetrated the core of his subconscious, setting in motion an irreversible process,

Without warning his body began to quake. The encrusted strata that formed the bedrock of his self now erupted with volcanic fury, spitting fragments of his past into a river of molten matter. When it had finally subsided, the Fool looked into the carnage. There, forged from the flames of his own reality, was the living sword of truth.

The Fool recognised the sword as his own integrity, which had arisen from the ashes of all that he had so far sacrificed. The justice of life, in accordance with his noble purpose, would now assist him in order that he be made more pure. But there was a price to be paid for such privilege: from here on, whenever he was untrue and faltered in his quest, he would bring hardship unto himself until the lessons of life were learned. The world could seize his possessions and even break his body, but his sword — his honour — could never be taken from him. In this he was a law unto himself, answerable only to the silence and stillness within him.

The Fool had invoked the supreme justice and was now responsible for his life as never before. Woman would preserve the cutting edge of his sword in existence. He had endeavoured to serve her, but now he was ready to confront and slay anything which would separate him from his beloved. She, in her unwavering devotion to love, would test his resolve; for it was his dishonesty to love that had upset the balance of the scales. The law of life decreed that the Fool must put right that which in his ignorance he had avoided: there was no greater Justice than this.

VIII

JUSTICE / LA JUSTICE

SYMBOLISM

Justice is a state of poise, the integrity of life that is represented by the unwavering equilibrium of the universe. It is seen in the order of nature, where every living thing in turn contributes to the survival of another in the cycle of life and death. Emanating from within, it is an impulse that compels an individual to do what he knows to be right for the situation, which may conflict with the world's idea of good and bad.

Justice is symbolised in the Tarot card by a figure holding a sword and scales. The sword is the power in man, his individual integrity. It is forged through the trials of existence, the experience of the precarious nature of the human condition. It often appears cold and impersonal, since it is unaffected by sentiment and emotionality. Its power functions entirely in the present as an inner reality that is not dependent on the past, or on anyone or anything in the external world. The scales are the measure of the value of an individual's life, recording the effects of the highs and lows of living that frequently upset the balance. It is often when the scales are sufficiently out of kilter that the individual is ready to look for the timeless justice within.

With the propaganda of the daily media, the knowledge that all is impeccably just can rarely be perceived through the apparent cruelty and exploitation in the world. Justice is to be responsible for all that I, the individual, have been. It is the realisation that my inner state is mirrored in my external life. By refusing to justify my anger or any other emotional negativity, a remarkable transformation can occur. In this moment, with the scales in perfect equilibrium, the idea of justice can be known, revealing itself in the pause that enables life to be perceived in the context of the whole. With this new perception and the willingness to accept life's adjudication, there is eventually a greater harmony both within and without.

In his Chariot, the Fool's noble purpose was revealed: to make amends for his betrayal of love on earth, the injustice of the ages. In invoking the sword of truth, he is now ready to take conscious responsibility for his life and begin to live with a sense of purpose beyond the consideration of personal self. The sword can only be drawn by he who is prepared to die to his self; for the scales of justice are balanced by love.

DIVINING JUSTICE

Justice is a mighty symbol in the Tarot, encapsulating the virtue and courage of an individual. Its true significance in an enquiry is often only revealed in time in the eternal justice of life.

As an OPENING card, the impersonal nature of Justice presents the opportunity to face oneself direct. This reveals the integrity of a situation and the action, should it be necessary, to rectify the balance of the scales. Justice can sometimes represent litigation.

As a card in ASSISTANCE, Justice indicates a state of poise and alertness. There is a balanced approach to the nature of the enquiry, with the ability to perceive the facts from a place of detachment. There can be a willingness to break with compromise or the injustice of a situation in order to do what is known to be right.

As an OPPOSING card, Justice may advise a pause to weigh up the situation before taking action. There is a need to face the facts, for what is desired may not be feasible at this time. There may be a lack of responsibility in some area, causing inertia and a distortion of perception.

As the OUTCOME of an enquiry, Justice can indicate a period of stability and an opportunity to reappraise a situation in the context of the whole. Although it may not be perceived immediately, it symbolises the harmonising of circumstances as a result of responsible action.

❄

THE HERMIT

THE MYTH OF THE HERMIT

The Hermit told the Fool that many such as he had been before him in search of the higher knowledge. Most were seekers for betterment and gain, and so were encrusted in matter to be eroded in the passage of time.

Both Hermit and Fool descended deep into the bowels of the earth. With only the light of the lamp to guide them, they eventually reached an opening, where the Hermit spent most of his life in silence and solitude. It was revealed that this was to be a time of withdrawal for the Fool, away from the distractions of the world. He was instructed to be watchful for any movement of his mind, as this would call up the ghosts of the past.

After a while, the lamp began to flicker and the Hermit faded from view. In the darkness a terrible feeling of isolation arose within the Fool. As his mind began to race, shadows of his long-forgotten fears manifested on the walls around him. They were the demons of the underworld, the imaginative creations of his past. The Fool was petrified. Like those before him it seemed that he was to remain a prisoner in time.

From deep within the blackness of his rigid body, he registered an energetic presence: there, once more, he beheld the sword of truth, the essence of his valour. Breaking free from the confinement of his ignorance and fear, he grasped the sword by the hilt. In that moment a flash of brilliant light filled the darkness. The Fool, now aglow, had illuminated his own lamp, and the phantoms had fled to their underworld.

The Hermit appeared once more. The Fool had earned the right to continue his journey, but was warned not to look back, for this would extinguish the flame. It would be his task to preserve the light of the lamp that would guide him deeper into the unknown.

VIIII

THE HERMIT / L'HERMITE

SYMBOLISM

Guided by the Hermit, the Fool has now entered the passage between the inner and outer worlds. There are many pitfalls, for this is the area of the subconscious which consists of the past emotional layers of unhappiness, solidified as the resistant matter of his self. With the illumination of his own lamp, he can now descend more swiftly back through time to the source of his own radiant inner sun.

In the Tarot card, the Hermit embodies the original seeker of truth. His lamp symbolises the light of intelligent reflection that enables him to penetrate the walls of himself. To begin with, he has to generate his own light. Its power is activated by containing the energy usually dissipated through the outer fixation with the material world. As the flame is frequently extinguished in this polluted atmosphere, there can be a need to withdraw from the superficial pleasures and habitual attachments of existence. His staff is that which supports him when his light is obscured by the fears and uncertainties that he encounters in his descent into the unknown.

The Hermit has now gone underground. In the western world there is no time or space for the devotional spirit. The traditional role of the Hermit was to live in seclusion. Whether as monk, mystic or sage, he found material convenience and the company of his fellow man intolerable, preferring to be alone in communion with his God; here he could preserve the light of his lamp, the knowledge of his own inner reality. However, with the outer forces of the progressive world pressing in on him, he was eventually absorbed by the gathering wave of intellectual enquiry and the formation of new scientific disciplines. Today his influence is found in the great seats of learning where, in the pursuit of knowledge outside himself, his true character has hardened into a mental aberration, with his vision now set on a virtual reality.

There is a time for the Fool to be alone, but he can no longer remain isolated in the exclusion of his love. By holding up his lamp to the ignorance of his self, he sees that he cannot return to what he has been. To parallel his deeper descent through the dark tunnel of himself, he must continue to discover the truth in the realisation of his love in existence. His lamp, his passion, is the light of consciousness that will guide him.

DIVINING THE HERMIT

The Hermit is the guiding light of the Tarot. Symbolising the yearning for a greater connection with the truth, he endeavours to draw the attention inwards wherever possible.

As an OPENING card, the Hermit highlights a specific area of the questioner's life. It could be something that has recently surfaced, or may have been the subject of reflection over a long period. There may be a need to withdraw temporarily from activity to evaluate changing events.

As a card in ASSISTANCE, the Hermit's lamp is sufficiently illuminated to focus on a situation without distraction. He can indicate that a period of reflection may be beneficial to investigate a matter at a deeper level.

In OPPOSITION, the Hermit shines his lamp on something that has been overlooked or an avoidance of responsibility. There may be a fear to face up to a situation, and the questioner may have psychologically withdrawn from the world. The emphasis is on a greater understanding of the facts of the matter and a deeper knowledge of oneself.

As the OUTCOME, it is a time when clearer insights may result in a change of outlook and an expansion of awareness. There can be the emergence of new opportunities through the courage to investigate areas previously obscured by the fears of the past. Whatever direction the questioner takes, the Hermit's lamp will act as a beacon to guide him towards his potential.

❄

THE WHEEL OF FORTUNE

THE MYTH OF THE WHEEL OF FORTUNE

The Fool observed the colourful images on the spinning Wheel of Fortune. Ever-changing scenes were enticing him to experience once again the pleasures of the world. With his lamp illuminated, he could now effect changes for his own self-interest and gain. The riches of the world would earn him the respect from those who, in their ignorance, had dared to dismiss him as a fool.

But what of woman, his love? She, of course, would share in his new-found wealth and rank, but many would be vying for his favours. Seduced by the endless possibilities, the Fool went around the Wheel again.

Unexpectedly, a tremor from the depths of the earth shook the entire structure of the Wheel. Cracks appeared in the ground as a torrent of water gushed forth, bringing with it the stench of the rotting carcasses that had been buried deep below. What had once been the delights of the world now took on a grotesque appearance.

The Fool struggled to hold on to the Wheel as it began to rotate more quickly. He observed that he was not alone, for along with him, in a frantic scramble to retain their grip on existence, was the entire human race. Those who hung on were compelled to keep moving at higher speed, before falling into the deluge below. The Fool finally realised he could do nothing: it was all a magnificent illusion. He had risen above the world.

The Wheel stopped. In that moment everything was in its place, including the Fool. Holding steady from his new vantage point above, he was free from its hypnotic pull. Any thought to change the world would set the Wheel in motion; for it was his restless mind that propelled it. With this knowledge came the strength to face the force within, the next challenge that awaited him.

X

LAROUE DE FORTUNE

X

THE WHEEL OF FORTUNE / LA ROUE DE FORTUNE

SYMBOLISM

The Fool, sufficiently detached from the falsity of his self, can now perceive the truth of the Wheel of Fortune – that it is the illusory world of the Magician. Separated from the mechanical whirl of the wheel, he realises that there is no fate, chance or apparent coincidence outside of his own individual integrity.

The Tarot card pictures two creatures on a wheel, with a strange figure above them. The wheel is the progressive world, whose momentum is maintained by the creatures on either side. They represent the human race, clinging to the two extremes of existence: the pleasure of attainment and the pain of loss. Human beings are programmed from birth to attach themselves to the wheel, regardless of the suffering endured. Propelled by the anticipation of new experiences and the repetition of the old, the wheel continues to turn, fuelling the continuous movement of the mind – the mechanical thought process which, devoid of love, seeks forever to understand its own creation. Eventually, when worn down by the constant repetition of existence, the individual may question the meaning of his life.

The figure above the wheel stands alone. He is an ideal which humanity is evolving towards, through the karma of endless living and dying. Remaining impassive to the activity on the wheel, he looks beyond the confines of mortal man to the deeper knowledge of life. In the absence of force, he observes without wanting to change anything; in this he is a Magician of higher consciousness, poised to serve love and life in the expression of his true creativity in the world. However, the addictive pull of the world is so great that he can remain in limbo, unable to realise his true potential. The temptation in his elevated position of power is to degrade the deeper mysteries of life to work his psychic magic. In exploiting his fellow man to serve and worship him, he is the most manipulative force in creation.

The Fool has realised that he is going nowhere on the Wheel of Fortune. Resisting the compulsion to attach himself to it again, he is committed to face the force in himself. Having seen that existence is only a temporary projection, he can gradually detach from the beliefs and notions that have separated him from his love; for in love there is no opposite and the wheel of thought is stilled.

DIVINING THE WHEEL OF FORTUNE

The Wheel of Fortune mirrors the uncertain nature of existence. It is an expansive symbol which challenges the individual to perceive the world, and his place in it, with a greater reality and purpose.

As an OPENING card, the Wheel of Fortune can symbolise changing events which may act as a springboard to enter a new cycle. It may be a time to re-evaluate one's life, and to take a chance to break with the habitual patterns of the old.

As a card in ASSISTANCE, there may be good fortune appearing as a new opportunity or material gain from an unexpected source. Here, circumstances can combine to assist the questioner in whatever he perceives as the fulfilment of his life.

In OPPOSITION, a rapid turn of events may lead to a period of disruption and confusion. This can be a challenge to the individual to face any self-deception or irresponsibility. There may be a need to break an attachment which is causing a leakage of energy.

As the OUTCOME, the Wheel of Fortune can symbolise the completion of a cycle. There may be a period of success and worldly recognition, and a sense of achievement. It can mirror a greater maturity and vision of life through the experience gathered in the world. What may have limited the questioner's creative potential in the past can now be seen to have been an illusion.

❄

FORCE

THE MYTH OF FORCE

Within the Fool, the beast was rampant. Prowling through the labyrinth of the Fool's subconscious mind, it was ready to pounce, alert to the slightest movement of the Wheel. Yet nothing appeared to be moving. Through the Fool's vigilance on the Wheel of Fortune, the beast was being starved. Now exposed as the force of his conflicting self, it was compelled to scavenge where, before, it could gorge to excess. Unable to satisfy its terrible hunger, the beast returned to its lair.

In the silence, the Fool could now detect a distant beat. The beast, in desperate need of sustenance, had changed its tactic. In the deep recesses of the Fool's subconscious, it had begun to pound the psychic drum of war: the ancient call of battle, the wild remnant of his fighting nature. Slowly succumbing to its hypnotic rhythm, the Fool was being drawn into the fray. The beast, salivating at the prospect of a certain banquet, quickened the beat of the drum.

As the psychic battle raged, the Fool fought to remain conscious, locked in a struggle against the brute force of his reactionary self. Roaring with the fury of the ages, the beast moved in for the kill. The Fool held his ground, facing the full onslaught of his foe as it tore blindly at his flesh. In excruciating pain, he grasped the beast by the jaws, containing the force which only the power of will could withstand.

Its feed denied, the beast finally withdrew. The Fool knew that it would be back; but from now on he would recognise its scent far more swiftly than before.

XI

LA FORCE

XI

FORCE / LA FORCE

SYMBOLISM

Man is distinguished from the rest of the species by a self-reflective capability that enables him to be conscious of himself as an individual identity. Yet this faculty of self-reflection allows his animal drive, which is the instinctive intelligence behind all living creatures, to forever seek expression through his body as his rampant sexual nature. This is the beast – the part of him that is wild.

A figure holds the jaws of a ferocious animal, which appears subdued. In some versions of the Tarot, the figure is portrayed as woman to accentuate the vanquishing of brute force through a subtlety of power that is not reliant on conflict or violence. This is the power of will, invoked by the individual through the nobility of purpose that transcends the fluctuating feelings of the personal self. The beast is the remnant of man's savage ancestry. Today, tamed by the comfort and convenience of the civilising process and attuned to the pendulum of living, the beast lies dormant, content to rest as a background vibration. However, when cornered or denied an emotional feed, it can erupt with a startling ferocity.

One obvious solution to combat the force of the beast, seen by many inspired by the love of the truth throughout the ages, was celibacy. By excluding woman, the celibate could starve the beast in himself, achieving inner union with his feminine part. Yet he could never be fully complete as man. In turning his back on woman, he not only denied himself the realisation of his love in existence, but was selfishly protective of his truth in his fear of God in female form.

The Fool must love externally as he continues to make the journey within, for it is woman who takes the force of his virulent sexual energy and converts it back to love. All that he has been as the accumulated negativity of the past must now come forward to be accounted for. This is an intense period, when only the love of something greater than himself can overcome the immemorial presence of the beast. The willing surrender of the person, the unhappy emotional self, brings the power that offers no resistance to the forces of creation: this is willpower, the hallmark of inner strength. Intrinsic to this is the acceptance of life as it is, as the pressure to be true intensifies in the ordeal of the Hangman.

DIVINING FORCE

The essence of Force is the power in the individual, the inner strength to master the reactions of negative emotions through an intelligent response to the situation.

As an OPENING card, Force can symbolise the power to confront the source of any emotional disturbance, and to withstand a period of intensity. This power is invoked through the willingness to face oneself and to take practical action, but without being drawn into any conflict in the situation.

As a card in ASSISTANCE, Force symbolises that there is the courage present within the questioner to overcome any obstruction or difficulty. There is a resolve and great stamina to withstand external forces in the knowledge of the rightness of one's actions.

In OPPOSITION, there may be a need for the containment of reactionary emotions. There could be a build-up of resistance to external circumstances. It is important to identify the source of any negativity within oneself to prevent unnecessary difficulties from arising.

As an OUTCOME, Force reveals the opportunity to realise one's inner strength and valour through a selfless love of the whole. The solution is within the questioner and, should the appropriate action be taken for what is known to be right, a new resource of vitality will be released.

❋

THE HANGMAN

The Myth of the Hangman

Wherever the Fool turned, there was nothing. He felt abandoned, suspended between two worlds, one drawing him in and the other pulling him out. Separated from the familiar movement of the Wheel of Fortune, and with the beast quiescent for now, the Fool was in the desert of himself.

The world seemed barren and devoid of love as he searched desperately for something familiar to hold on to. Clutching at the remnants of his past, he felt a tug of emotional pain and severe discomfort within his body. Life was demanding the ultimate sacrifice: the voluntary surrender of his self.

The Fool's world had been turned upside down. A devastating feeling of emptiness made him yearn for the reassuring embrace of the mother and the nourishing warmth of the womb. Looking within, he perceived the cord that bound him to his pain, which in his ignorance he had mistaken for love. As he lunged at the cord its grip tightened, attaching him more firmly than ever to existence. The crushing inner pressure was stretching him to the limit of endurance.

There was a long period of aridity while the Fool valiantly accepted his ordeal. He had seen, through the absence of experience, that the purpose of his suffering was to break his attachment to the pain of personal love. In his surrender to the great impersonal God within, he realised that it was this that he loved so dearly.

The Fool watched as the cord attaching him to existence was released. As he descended into the earth, the reality inside his body, an extraordinary energy was arising from the depths to meet him. He was travelling into uncharted territory, yet it was recognisable as something he knew: it was the unmistakable presence of Death.

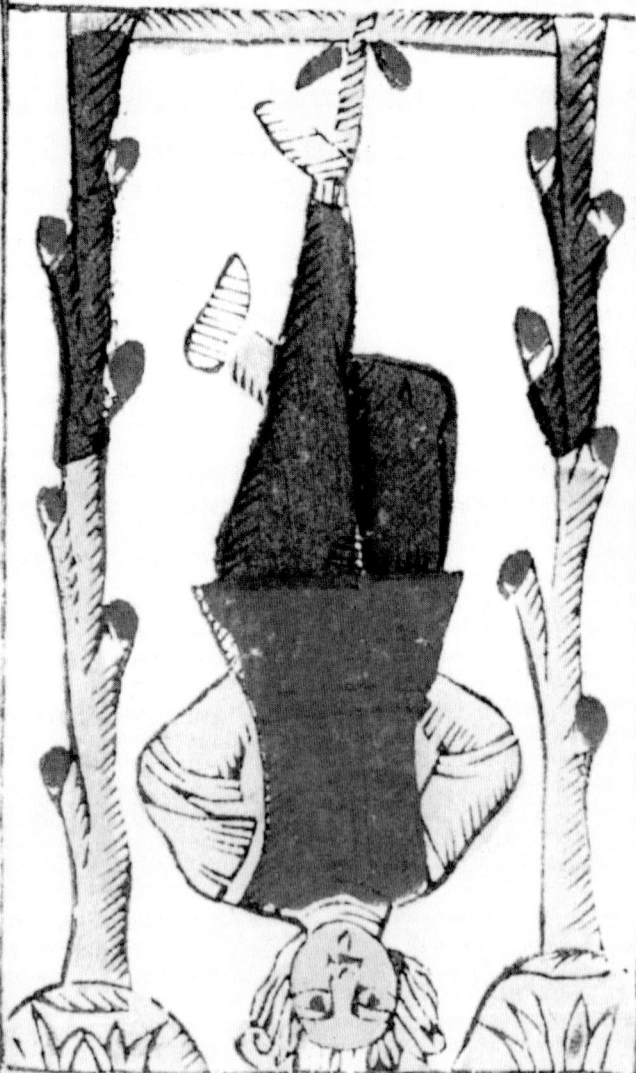

LE PENDU

XII

THE HANGMAN / LE PENDU

SYMBOLISM

The Hangman symbolises the crossing of the threshold, the point of no return. Initiated by the Hermit, the Fool now undergoes a period of self-abnegation, when only the love of something greater than himself can give him the power to endure his ordeal. Through his self-sacrifice, the light of intelligence is now able to penetrate the deeper layers of resistance in the subconscious, and he can descend further into the profundity of his being.

In the Tarot card, a figure is pictured upside down, suspended by a rope from the gallows. He looks out towards the world from his strange reversed perspective in gracious acceptance of his ordeal. The starkness of the upright limbs symbolises the severing of personal love, the sentimental attachment that bound him to the past. They are existing with the minimum of sustenance, yet the roots are firmly embedded in the earth. Likewise, the Hangman is deeply rooted in the inner life, with his focus directed inwards towards the source of his own reality.

The Hangman is the symbol of the devotional love of the unknown. Through the negation of his self, the Fool serves the great impersonal; this purifies his sexual momentum – the beast he is endeavouring to master. While there is still the emotional residue of the past, he must endure the purifying process, converting the raw energy of emotion into a finer expression of love. To purify his body, through which the inner journey is made, he must surrender his attachment to the world in the selfless offering of the inner alms to love.

To an observer, the Hangman may appear condemned to suffer an appalling fate in the loss of his freedom. This will be avoided at all costs by those still attached to the Wheel of Fortune. It is a time of aridity, when the absence of worldly experience exerts a terrible pressure on the individual to withstand the state of nothing. However, man who is ready goes voluntarily to the gallows. He knows that to be truly free, the emotional content of his personal self must die. In the struggle to separate from the ignorance of the past, the thread attaching him to existence can appear to tighten, stretching him towards a new perception of life. Woman endures the ordeal with him, surrendering for her man to unite her once more with the earth, her untarnished ground of love.

DIVINING THE HANGMAN

The essence of the Hangman is self-surrender. It is the willingness to have one's whole world turned upside down, if necessary, to give up the attachment to the emotional negativity of the past.

As an OPENING card, the Hangman symbolises the opportunity for the questioner to examine a situation from a different perspective. It can symbolise an ordeal of some kind in which voluntary personal sacrifice may be involved.

As a card in ASSISTANCE, the Hangman reflects the willingness to endure a situation in the surrender of personal consideration. There can be an acceptance of any hardship in the knowledge that what is being endured is of great value to the whole.

In OPPOSITION, the Hangman symbolises a lengthy ordeal that may require absolute dedication and resolve to overcome. There may be a change in circumstances, challenging one's ability to adapt. It can indicate a period of inactivity, which needs to be endured before the true purpose of a situation can be ascertained.

As the OUTCOME, there is the knowledge that what is being undertaken is necessary, even though from a worldly perspective it could be condemned as foolhardy. There is often great virtue in the ordeal of the Hangman, which can reveal the essence of the questioner's character.

❄

DEATH

THE MYTH OF DEATH

Death had entered the Fool. At first its presence was felt as a jolt of primal power which sent his body into physical contortion. Sometimes the energy would distort his features and make him almost unrecognisable; at other times it remained as a background vibration. The effect on his self was exhausting.

The Fool had died many times on his journey. Some of these deaths had been more painful than others, but each had served to bring him closer to the truth of life and the freedom from his attachment to the world. The burden of sorrow and despair that he had carried for so long could be endured no more. Through his willingness to give his life to the service of love, the process had intensified. Death had been invoked and would now be relentless in its purging of his past.

The Fool's body began to shudder as he descended into a turbulent band of the psyche. In the terrible confusion, he withstood the buffeting of the transformative power. He was now a passenger beyond space and time, expanding and contracting with the cyclic pulse of life.

Resisting no longer the cleansing energy of Death, the Fool watched as the coarse weeds of emotion that had choked his joy of life were scythed with merciless precision. The release was ecstatic as the sap of life, no longer dammed, flowed freely through his being.

The Fool had entered the mystery of Death and was vitally alive as never before. Yet he could not remain in this exalted state of consciousness, for his journey was far from over. He would now have to live with its extraordinary energy and die continually to his residual self in the pursuit of his noble quest.

XIII

DEATH / LA MORT

SYMBOLISM

Death is the cleansing energy of life, a shedding of all that has been. It is vitally present, transforming all things in creation with the immediacy of every new moment. The journey of the Fool is the conscious dying to his self. It is an inner death, a psychological and emotional purging which begins with the dawning of maturity when the impermanence of living is perceived.

In the Tarot card, the reaper, the traditional personification of death, is seen scything his field. The skeleton of man, stripped to the bone of his beliefs and concepts, is revealed in all its animal rawness. Death is a cosmic energy whose effect is seen in existence in the purging and decomposition of matter. In the field are two severed heads: the crowned head represents the sun, the projective male principle of life coming into existence; the female head symbolises the moon, the receptivity of the female principle and the cyclic flow of life returning to the earth.

Death is the ultimate mystery of life, the apparent fate that awaits all things born in existence. Yet it is only man, in the false identification with the physical body as his own reality, who fears the inevitable: the return journey to whence he came. The Fool was once in touch with death, in intimate connection with the inner and outer worlds – the two hemispheres of existence. This natural state of equilibrium was preserved in the presence of love. In today's loveless world the innocence of the newborn is inevitably corrupted, and the knowledge of death is concealed through the fear and neurosis of society.

Love is the bridge that enables man to journey ever closer towards his immortal reality. Death is the daily dying for love, the constant surrender of negative emotions. It is the giving up of position and the refusal to justify anger; it is the dying to fluctuating feelings and to be true to the situation at all times; and it is the courage to accept life as it is. Once invoked, the death energy is relentless in its task: to purge the individual of his attachments to the world. It can be a painful and disorientating process while there is resistance in the matter through the holding on to the ignorance of the past. Yet there is the knowledge that to realise the truth of death while still alive is to be connected with the joy of life for ever.

DIVINING DEATH

In the Tarot, Death reflects the inevitability of change and the opportunity to sever the ties to the past. It is the process of allowing the vital movement of life to express itself as the new.

As an OPENING card, Death is powerfully placed to cleanse and transform, whether in the facing of an inner emotional conflict or external crisis. It can indicate the need to sever an attachment, either to a person or a situation. There may be an intense period of adjustment if there is resistance to the process of change.

As a card in ASSISTANCE, Death symbolises a wave of renewal. There can be the opportunity to make a clean break with a situation that no longer serves, and the energy to adapt to changes which could be beneficial.

In OPPOSITION, Death usually indicates a major challenge to overcome. This will test the individual's resolve to the limit of endurance, but may bring about a complete transformation of character. When there is resistance to accept the end of a natural cycle, there can be a build-up of sluggish energy, distorting perception and severely depleting resources.

As an OUTCOME, Death can symbolise the potential for a total transformation, and the completion of a significant phase of one's life. With this comes the resurgence of power and the freedom to move on to the nourishment of the new.

❄

TEMPERANCE

The Myth of Temperance

Death had transformed the Fool. It had been a traumatic process as he adjusted to its energetic presence. His new lightness of being, however, had soon become heavy with the residue of all that had been released, and now a grainy sediment of self was restricting the flow of life. Depleted of vitality, he was in dire need of replenishment.

Descending into the blackness of inner space, he entered a place of extraordinary tranquillity. There he beheld a vision, a manifestation from the angelic realm. She had appeared as a symbol of the Fool's increasing sensitivity to love. Such was her purity that it was agonising for him to gaze upon her. Enveloped by her ethereal beauty, the Fool merged with the angelic presence as her energy permeated his every cell. The virtue of all that had been sacrificed thus far could now be refined and distilled as the essence of his life.

It was a time of nourishment and wonder for the Fool. Connected to the purity of his being, he saw that he was life without form, an endless stream of impersonal love. With no impediment in himself to hinder its flow, he was in harmony with all things in existence in an eternal cycle of giving and receiving.

The vision receded. It had been a simple, yet profound, communication. Revitalised by the purification of Temperance, the Fool would now have to go on. It would be crucial to contain the timeless essence within him in preparation for what was to come: the diabolical encounter with his self.

XIIII

TEMPERANCE

XIIII

TEMPERANCE / TEMPERANCE

SYMBOLISM

Temperance, as a symbol of the harmonious flow of life on earth, refines and extracts the impurities of existence in a continuous distilling process. The natural order is maintained through the law of magnetism, in which the two opposite poles draw to each other whatever is necessary to preserve the balance of life.

In the Tarot card, a woman is portrayed as an angel, symbolising a purified state of being. In her hands are two containers, through which she filters the stream of life. Processing the pleasure and pain of the living experience, she harmonises the energies of the masculine and feminine principles into one divine essence, enabling love to travel free of the impediment of force.

The mind of man is permanently active, even in sleep, and virtually impossible to disengage at will. This distorts the magnetic field of Temperance and repels the natural flow of life, creating the problematical world which is mirrored in the pollution of the earth.

Negative emotions form a psychic dam, exerting great pressure from within. This is inevitably released in some form of over-indulgence, such as sexual promiscuity, alcohol or drugs. A depletion of vitality usually follows, accompanied by depression and self-doubt, and the pattern is repeated in an effort to re-experience the emotional high.

The purifying essence of Temperance is registered in the individual in certain climacterics of life. Puberty is the signal for the floodgates to be opened for the surge of reproductive energy to enter the system. This is later refined in maturity, appearing in woman as the cycle of the menopause and, often, in man as a mid-life crisis. This is sometimes seen as a conscious re-evaluation of all that has so far been experienced and a discarding of that which no longer serves.

Death was the catalyst needed to break through the resistance of the Fool, enabling Temperance to manifest from the energetic point of his inner reality. This set in motion the purification process that would allow him to descend deeper into the mystery of life through an increasing sensitivity to love. He is now poised, nourished by the rejuvenating flow, in preparation for what is to come. His task is to continue to dismantle his self so that he can consciously merge with the energy of Temperance in an uninterrupted state of love.

DIVINING TEMPERANCE

Temperance, as an expression of love and purity, brings a sense of harmony to a reading. Symbolising the attraction of opposites, she endeavours wherever possible to correct any energy imbalance.

As an OPENING card, Temperance can symbolise a time of reflection after an upheaval of some kind. There may be the need to contain one's energy during a period of adjustment to new circumstances.

As a card in ASSISTANCE, there can be a resurgence of vitality and a connection with one's well-being. In this placement, Temperance can symbolise a steady, calming influence, enabling the questioner to take action in areas which may hitherto have been impenetrable or blocked.

In OPPOSITION, there is the possibility of energy leakage due to a stressful situation or over-indulgence in some area. If this continues, there is likely to be a depletion of resources and the need for a period of recuperation.

As an OUTCOME, there is a process of purification at work. There is now a containment of energy, allowing a smooth transition from one sequence to the next. All that has been experienced can be refined for the true value to be deemed, manifesting as a harmonious flow of events.

❄

THE DEVIL

The Myth of the Devil

Darkness was upon the Fool. Catching sight of his reflection, he recoiled: his face had twisted into a sneering mask, and staring out of the eyes was the diabolical effigy of his self.

The Fool was appalled by what he saw, for here was the Magician's shadow, the seething presence of his demonic craving for power. Coarse and ignoble, it was the treacherous tenant that lurked behind every man on earth. Cruel and cunning, it stalked the innocent and plagued the guilty, a ruthless predator and a master of disguise.

The Fool had descended into hell. There waiting to greet him was the Devil, oozing with seductive charm. He offered the Fool the world: as a Magician of unlimited power, he would create as never before, answerable only to the Devil himself. Together they would gorge on the spoils of humanity in a never-ending orgy of lust.

Tormented by the fiendish energy, the Fool was plunging deeper into hell. The remnants of his dishonesty to love were now swirling in his mind in a maelstrom of unbridled excitement. The Devil, bloated and obscene, urged him to discharge the pent-up psychic force so that he could possess his body once more. On the verge of submission, the Fool resisted any movement of his mind to indulge in the shameful sordidness of his past, and endured the scalding heat of the cauldron.

The Devil had been thwarted; his very existence was now threatened. Inflamed by hatred and loathing, he assailed the Fool with mocking abuse in a desperate attempt to drag him down to purgatory again. Unable to manipulate the psychic space between them, the Devil was powerless to possess him.

It was over. The Fool watched as the entity withdrew, banished forever. He had finally severed his ties with his adversary – and his oldest friend.

XV

LE DIABLE

XV

THE DEVIL / LE DIABLE

SYMBOLISM

The Devil's possession of humanity is now global. Intimately known as the doubter and worrier, it sucks the innocence from the child and casts its bleak shadow across the radiance of youth. Entrenched in the adult as the incessant thinker, the Devil is stimulated by the deluge of information and entertainment transmitted twenty-four hours a day; yet it is still unable to be satisfied in its terrible craving for experience. The Devil of course is sex.

Appearing in the Tarot in traditional guise, the Devil is seen looming over two figures who, as man and woman, are tethered to his cauldron. Here, stripped of the Magician's finery, the projective outer reflection of the person is revealed in negative mode in all its emotional hardness and lusting. With the illusion shattered, there is no need for pretence or pleasantries as the diabolical entity is exposed. The cauldron is the pit of unhappiness, the inexhaustible ferment of hell on earth that chains man to the perverse need to re-experience his own pain.

Unable to equate humanity's lovelessness and diabolical nature with the workings of the one God, the religionists declared that man's evil deeds were the work of something outside himself – the great Satan. By the usurpation of pagan deities of earlier cultures (deemed as suitable demonic effigies), the priests could now justify man's shortcomings and vices as something unworldly, and impossible to be responsible for. Mirroring their own lack of love and devilish propensity, the priests indoctrinated the people with the notion of hellfire and damnation. Through the fear, guilt and superstition engendered, the Devil was fully established as the scapegoat of humanity, an invention of the church to give credence to the atrocities of living.

Today the invitation of the Devil is extended to all through the seduction of glossy magazines, video, computer and the news of the world. With a plethora of choice to distract man from his restlessness and discontent, the violence of his diabolical energy is dispersed through innumerable outlets. For those most vulnerable to the Devil's enticement, the build-up of force is often discharged through sexual excitement, masturbation, or some other form of self-gratification.

The Fool is here to make amends. In banishing the Devil, he is no longer chained to the emotional cravings of his personal self. That much closer to the source of his reality, he has now earned the right to enter the House of God.

DIVINING THE DEVIL

The Devil symbolises the potential for the shedding of the false. As the face of dishonesty, it can be a harsh reflection, exposing the rawness of oneself beneath the superficial sheen of the personality.

As an OPENING card, the Devil can symbolise the holding on to a past hurt or disappointment, especially in the realm of love. This may be casting its shadow over current circumstances in the form of resentment, jealousy or frustration.

As a card in ASSISTANCE, it gives the opportunity to look into the mirror of oneself to expose the deep inhibitions of the past. The Devil is a powerful force, usually requiring some form of personal sacrifice to confront it. In this placement there is the necessary energy to do this, but it may mean the breaking with some form of self-indulgence.

In OPPOSITION, the Devil may indicate a period of severe frustration in the unfoldment of a situation. In a relationship, it can symbolise a build-up of emotional negativity and lack of communication. Unless there is great resolve to face the situation without a distortion of the facts, the solution may be blocked.

As an OUTCOME, the Devil can symbolise a tremendous overcoming and the end of compromise. Through the courage to take action to free oneself from the emotional bondage of the past, there can be the purification of stagnant emotions such as guilt or self-doubt.

❄

THE HOUSE OF GOD

The Myth of the House of God

The Devil, the lascivious tenant, had gone. After the initial sense of liberation had receded, a sadness had come upon the Fool, casting a shadow over his inner light. He wept penitent tears which cleansed the shame of his deeds that had once dishonoured the earth.

The Fool was on the edge of existence, waiting in the solitude that encompassed him. Becoming aware of a gathering uneasiness, he perceived that his body was a tower, earthed to receive the elemental charge of God. Flashes of lightening forked through the night sky as a storm broke in the heavens. Suddenly it struck, and a bolt of supernal energy thundered through his body. In the electrified space, the deadening matter buried in the recesses of his subconscious mind was shattered by the destructive charge of creation.

In the silence that followed, the Fool saw that where there had been something, there was now nothing. Descending into the stillness of the void, he knew a peace beyond his understanding. Yet on the perimeter of his mind there was an energy imposing itself on this sacred space.

Now, from deep within his being, came a surge of spiritual power, expelling from their captive quarters in the bowels of the earth the hardened emotional prisoners of time. Erupting from the Fool in a spiralling vortex were the fragments of the immemorial past that had been grafted on the body of humanity, purged at last of their turgid negativity.

Finally, when it seemed that nothing remained, the Fool sank into the silent space within. Emptied of the impurities of the world, he was now worthy to enter this holy domain as a shining exemplar in the House of God.

XVI

LA MAISON DIEU

XVI

THE HOUSE OF GOD / LA MAISON DIEU

SYMBOLISM

From the outside, the destructive energy of the House of God can be devastating – a thunderbolt which can shatter the foundation of all that has been secure. In the aftermath, the shocking disruption of life is rarely perceived as positive; the vacuum created is quickly filled by the emotions, and the opportunity to look into reality is lost. The Fool has entered the House of God from the inside, and through his spiritual preparation is now able to contain its primal power.

In the Tarot card, a bolt of great energy raises the lid of a crowned turret. The tower is the purifying chamber of the body. The two figures seen plummeting towards the ground symbolise the two creative principles, man and woman, now liberated from the confines of the Devil's cauldron. The release from bondage has set in motion a dramatic chain of events. A spiritual charge has penetrated the core of resistance, releasing a build-up of inner pressure. The circular boulders symbolise the effect of spirit entering matter, discharging the fragments of negative energies to be purified. In the continuing cyclic process the body becomes a passage, free of impediment, permitting a deeper descent into the profundity of inner space.

The House of God as the temple of humanity is now desecrated by the pollution of the world and, its defences fortified, is no longer vulnerable to love. Through the worship of orgasm – the false god of existence – the House of God is short-circuited, degenerating the passion of love into the excitement of sex. The moment of release is represented by the splitting of the atom, and the fall-out disseminated on the earth as the misery and conflict of existence.

Today, divided from the true authority of the Emperor, man is separated from the consciousness of his phallus, the original magical wand of the Magician. His deepest longing is to be able to contain the sheer beauty of woman. It is the fear to love to his full capacity that separates him from his true creative genius: it is his task to purify his body to be worthy of entry into the powerhouse of love. In truly loving woman in the surrender of his selfish need for release, his sexual nature is refined. The fusion of the two creative principles of man and woman can then be contained in the flesh to produce a divine consciousness, the essence of the House of God.

DIVINING THE HOUSE OF GOD

Traditionally viewed as a symbol of catastrophe and impending disaster, the House of God, in reality, represents a tremendous potential for self-change and spiritual awakening.

As an OPENING card, the House of God can often mirror an intense period of personal drama and upheaval, which may be shaking the foundation of what was apparently securely. This can be a cathartic process, if the questioner is willing to adapt and to take a greater responsibility for life.

As a card in ASSISTANCE, it indicates the ability to respond to changing events and the courage to take effective action under pressure. It can signal a breakthrough of some kind and the end of a period of frustration.

In OPPOSITION, the House of God can signal a sudden change in a situation and the possible disruption of circumstances. In some instances this can be extreme, requiring a steady, practical approach to overcome any negative influence.

As the OUTCOME, the House of God can symbolise the liberation from a self-imposed prison. There can be a release of deeply-held beliefs and concepts which have blocked the true expression of love. Here, there is the energy to break the solid structures erected during the early formative years. To enter the House of God is to confront oneself direct. It can symbolise the end of all compromise, heralding a major change in the questioner's life.

❄

THE STAR

THE MYTH OF THE STAR

The Fool had entered a different realm. In a state of wonder, he perceived in its formless energetic splendour all that he had ever loved as the earth. No longer was he bound to the changing world of the senses, which were but a reflection in existence of the beauty that could never be tarnished within.

Carried on a wave of consciousness towards the knowledge of his own resplendent reality, the Fool was constantly nourished by the cosmic stream of life. Intimations of a vastness beyond his understanding expanded his vision to encompass the entire universe. Through the pristine clarity of space, he could now receive something that had eluded him for so very long: it was his own radiant star. From a deep constellation within, its light pulsed with cosmic brilliance, signalling his place in the supreme order of the cosmos.

After all that the Fool had so far endured on his journey, this was truly a taste of freedom; yet a subtle trepidation was now being registered within him. The turbulence began to escalate as he sensed the presence of a great mass, stirring from within the depths of the blackness. He looked to the star for guidance; but a veil obscured his vision. A feeling of dread arose as he realised his quest was not yet over, for he would now have to cross the threshold towards a greater reality: the realm of the unconscious mind.

Suddenly the Fool found himself locked in a different trajectory. Helpless to resist the unseen gravitational force, he was being pulled deep into the space of the unknown. Now clearly visible in the distance was a luminous orb: it was the awesome presence of the Moon.

XVII

THE STAR / L'ESTOILE

SYMBOLISM

The Fool's intelligence is now swift enough to see through the solidity of matter and the world of cause and effect. In the presence of the Star, he is able to withdraw at will into a more profound area of the psyche. The fleeting manifestation of Temperance, unable to sustain itself in the sluggish time frame of existence, was the necessary catalyst that opened him to a greater connection with the radiant point of consciousness within. The natural flow of life can now bypass the discursive mind and be received direct in the purified body of love.

In the Tarot card, a woman sits by a pool with a cluster of stars above her. Her nakedness symbolises the state of pure receptivity in which she is harmoniously attuned to the earth and the cosmos. Her containers are constantly replenished by the cosmic stream of life, cleansing any impurity in a perpetual cycle of giving and receiving. The central star is the eternal essence of man, guiding him from behind the scenes to realise his creative potential. The seven surrounding stars represent the supreme order and harmony of the universe. They are facets of the one star and, in ascending luminosity and brilliance, contribute to the activation of the nucleus of power. On a tree is a bird, the symbol of man's immortal being, freed at last from the cage of his limited vision and able to soar to the heavens as his own cosmic reality.

Everybody is a gathering star, a unique expression of life, which is realised on earth through the courage to be true to the inner being. When the mind is sufficiently stilled, the Star is illuminated and intimations of original knowledge may be received. This is sometimes expressed in the world through the genius of the individual inspired by the muse of the arts or science. Finally, when everything has been communicated as a representation of love, all that is seen to remain is its purity.

The Fool's journey is the descent through inner space to the central star, the idea of love itself. In the containment of his energy resources, he can travel at increasing speed towards the realisation of his own potential. He is now rapidly consuming his past in the shedding of all that he has been. Gravitating towards the immense power of his star, he must next pass through the orbit of the moon, the gateway to his own reality.

DIVINING THE STAR

The Star is the pristine symbol of higher consciousness. Drawn towards the harmony of the universe, the individual may experience a sense of joy and renewed vitality.

As an OPENING card, the Star can symbolise a receptive state in which an idea can now be practically applied in the world. There can be the presence of mental alertness and a clear perception of the situation. There may be new inspiration, or an insight into something which has been previously obscured by mental fatigue or emotional tension.

As a card in ASSISTANCE, the Star can symbolise originality and the activation of free-flowing ideas. There can be a renewal of resources through a process of internal cleansing, with a potential for a change of lifestyle. This may reveal itself as a need for a greater compatibility with one's surroundings, or possibly a change of diet.

In OPPOSITION, there is a possibility of mental and physical exhaustion through overwork, excitement or anxiety. There may be a need to withdraw from a situation in order to identify the source of the depletion.

As an OUTCOME, the Star clearly indicates a sense of nourishment from a situation. There can be great potential for a hidden value to be discerned which would enhance the life of the questioner. This can signal the advancement into a new area of life, which can now be entered with confidence in the knowledge that the ground has been well prepared.

❄

THE MOON

The Myth of the Moon

The Moon, serene in all her cosmic beauty, looked on impassively at the Fool. Gazing in awe, he knew that to proceed would take him beyond the bridge of mortality into the profound mystery of life. With the hazy presence of the Star beckoning him through the lunar veil, he began the perilous crossing.

Two creatures now appeared, unleashed from the deep unconscious, their howls an echo of the Fool's primeval past. They were the guardians of the gateway to his cosmic reality, the reflection of the savage forces that had clawed and battled for survival on the surface of the earth. Confrontation was nigh; yet the Fool could not succumb, for he had seen the futility of conflict. His power was in his wisdom, and he walked through unscathed.

Continuing further across the bridge, he sensed a stirring in the fathomless pool below. There lurked the monster, the nightmare companion of the child. Feeling the emergence of an unspeakable dread, the Fool watched as it surfaced from the depths: it was the manifestation of his self in its terrifying enormity. Engulfed by waves of shocking intensity that magnified whatever fear remained in his mind, he could feel his life force draining away.

As oblivion came towards him, the Fool perceived a glimmer of light in the core of his being. It began to glow more brightly as he reached towards its beauteous splendour. The essence of the Moon herself was illuminating his path, and he turned to face the hideous entity once more. Now he realised that, with no past to hold him back and no future to fear, he could step through the monster he had created as the illusion of himself.

It was done. He had crossed over the threshold to the other side. No longer could he be bound by the limitations of his mortal being. Spiralling outwards from beyond the orbit of the Moon, the Fool journeyed on towards the majesty of the Sun.

XVIII

LA LUNE

XVIII

THE MOON / LA LUNE

SYMBOLISM

Since ancient times, the moon's influence on the rhythm and flow of life has been seen to be of great significance in the relationship between man and the natural world. As a cosmic symbol of the serenity of the female principle, its true essence is often twisted by the human psyche into an object of superstition and fear.

In the Tarot card, the full moon is illuminated in the night sky. On a bridge, two animals appear in apparent confrontation. They symbolise the conflicting nature of man, his instinctive animal drive expressed through the sediment of negative emotions. The creature in the pool below is man's unconscious identity. Summoned by the moon, it rises to the surface, where its primordial energy influences humanity through the lunar veil of distortion. This is the dread of the unknown which lurks in everybody until the truth of life is perceived. The fortified castle towers represent the rigid outer shell of man, the hardened emotions that cling to the security of the past, holding back his true potential. It can often take the devastating energy of the House of God to prise open the turrets.

The moon's effect on the individual is very powerful, especially in the formative years when first impressions are registered by the developing mind. Encouraged by the parents and those in the immediate environment, the intelligence of the child is drawn out from its natural state of well-being into the external world of stimuli. The purity of the lunar energies, which kept the child finely attuned to the essence of nature, is then corrupted. With the child's growing dependence on his memory and imagination, a substitute world is created and, in time, the identification with his emotions as himself.

In his descent into the psyche, the Fool has travelled back through the subconscious as the distance from the earth to the moon. Since the beginning of the journey his vision has been obscured by the illusory lunar veil. This was the false identity with his self, the time that he had gathered in existence, which could only be dissolved by the severing of his emotional attachment to the world. In crossing the threshold into his immortal reality, the Fool has realised the Moon in all its radiant beauty, and is now free to travel deeper into the cosmos towards the glory of the Sun.

DIVINING THE MOON

The Moon is a powerful mirror, reflecting the deep waters of the subconscious. It can bring to the surface the hidden anxieties of the past, which may have been absorbed within the family orbit and even during gestation in the womb.

As an OPENING card, the Moon can symbolise an unwillingness to let go of dependence, not only on the mother but also associations formed in childhood. It is possible that there has been a sense of duty or a pressure to conform in a certain way, from which has arisen guilt and other emotional negativity.

As a card in ASSISTANCE, it symbolises that the questioner is now poised to break the orbit of a situation that has been stifling his true creative potential. Here, the Moon illuminates a specific area where there has been emotional manipulation and compromise. There is now the opportunity to cross the bridge into the new.

In OPPOSITION, the presence of the Moon can be oppressive, producing a feeling of extreme vulnerability. It is possible that this is linked to emotional conflict in a family situation or with someone in the immediate environment. There can be a need to sever one's ties, with a change of location, if necessary, to break the lunar orbit.

As an OUTCOME, the Moon symbolises the freedom from the emotionality of the past. This can be the beginning of a new phase of life, and the realisation that something of immense value has been achieved through the courage to let go of sentimental love and attachment.

❄

THE SUN

THE MYTH OF THE SUN

In his immortal being, the Fool could now delight in the simplicity and wonder of life as never before. Yet he was still not complete, for there was a residue of self within him that separated him from the fullness of his love.

Since journeying beyond the Moon into the vastness of the solar system, he had been gravitating towards the power of the Sun. This mighty nucleus of pure creativity now summoned him to come forward to meet his own reality. Shielding himself from the full glare of its radiance, he moved tentatively towards its centre.

Suddenly a terrible fear arose that formed an impenetrable wall, and he could go no further. He had come so far, and now it seemed he was to be denied the fulfilment of his quest. The Fool was finished, for he could not live in separation from his love, the divine union with the Creator God. Life was demanding the ultimate sacrifice: the surrender of the deepest core of his self. He stepped into the furnace to endure his baptism of fire, for only the pure of heart could enter the shrine of love; and now his time had come.

Fusing with his inner light, he began to glow as the scorching heat burned through his remaining resistance. In an instant he was engulfed by the flames as he turned to face the full glare of the Sun. The Fool watched above the screams of agony as the last bastion of his self was obliterated, and the barrier was no more. He was as nothing, yet within him the Sun was ablaze.

The Fool walked through into the Garden of Paradise. There, waiting, was his beloved, now eternally united with him in love.

XVIIII

THE SUN / LE SOLEIL

SYMBOLISM

The Sun is the symbol of light, the one universal being that is the brilliance of life within everybody on earth. Man, as the projective principle in existence, replicates its ceaseless giving in whatever he serves in the world as the demonstration of his love.

In the Tarot card, the Sun is magnificently aglow, the sire of life on earth. Its solar rays bathe two children standing in front of a wall in a scene of great purity. The children in their nakedness symbolise the unity of love and the return to innocence. Here the Holy Trinity is consecrated in eternal betrothal, with the unifying of the male and female principles as the realisation of the one divine consciousness of the Father Sun. Surrounding the Garden of Paradise is a wall of bricks. This has been erected in time by the rational mind to form an almost impenetrable barrier of past. Entry into the Garden, the timeless state of love, is only possible in the absence of wanting and trying, when the restless mind is stilled.

As the East represents containment and an inner state of poise, so the West is expressive, dispersing its energy in the changing conditions of the consumer age. The sun is always rising in the East. It is everlasting life, giving of itself in every new moment and holding on to nothing in the newest expression of its love. The setting sun is the symbol of the diminishing light of the western world. It disappears into the cyberspace, diffusing man's consciousness and exchanging it for his virtual reality, the shadow on the face of the earth.

The Fool's lamp was ignited through his resolve to discover something more real and enduring than the fleeting presence of the material world. The illumination of the lamp, the light of his human intelligence, had to be guided back to its source – the radiant inner sun. This journey into the nucleus of power was the most arduous undertaking of all time as the residual core of his self was finally consumed in the fire of its eternal flame.

The Fool has made the divine connection with this point of supreme creativity. Having realised the inner sun as the truth of himself, his purpose now is to bring that extraordinary energy into the divided world of man and woman. There he must now live his truth to enable the virtue of his journey to be evaluated as the judgement of his life.

DIVINING THE SUN

In the Tarot, the Sun challenges the individual to break free from the lunar attachments of the past to realise his true potential. Its radiance is able to penetrate to the core of the matter, whatever the nature of the enquiry.

> As an OPENING card, the brilliance of the Sun can symbolise a period of inspiration and the movement towards an expression of love in some form. It can indicate a stepping forward into the spotlight with the burning desire, hitherto unrealised, to do something unique to fulfil one's true potential.

> As a card in ASSISTANCE, the Sun provides extraordinary energy for the practical application of one's creativity. There is an ability to bring together all available resources to initiate action, and the capacity to complete an undertaking with passion and originality.

> In OPPOSITION, the Sun challenges an individual to break through his wall of resistance to face a situation that may be unfulfilling. It symbolises that there is sufficient solar power to shine through any limitations, even though the questioner's source of inspiration may be temporarily obscured.

> As the OUTCOME, the Sun symbolises the passion within the questioner to realise his true creative potential and the fulfilment of his desires. In this placement, there is a clear indication of the rightness of intended action.

❄

JUDGEMENT

THE MYTH OF JUDGEMENT

The Fool had realised the Sun of himself. He was now a cosmic beacon, radiating his joyousness to all who could receive it, in his devotion to the glory of life. As he wandered through the land, he observed with fascination the predicament and daily toil of his fellow man.

One day, the Fool entered a settlement where many people had gathered to receive the wisdom of his life. It was not unusual for those attracted by his divine presence to seek his guidance. A man came forward to tell of a life driven by greed that had brought him nothing but misery and travail; next came a beggar, wretched and untouchable; a cut-throat described how he had murdered and robbed to satisfy his violent impulses; a crippled old woman told of her hardship and suffering, for she had been the victim of despicable crimes.

There were many, many people from different creeds; each had come to the Fool to be judged for the virtue of his life. Yet he realised that these people were his former self, appearing in a different space and time. He was now both the judge and the judged. Although he had lived many lives, in truth there was but one life; and now, finally, he was complete, enlightened of his ignorance of the past. All things had served his awakening: the apparent good and the bad. It was a profound moment as he merged with the vast knowledge of all that he had ever been.

The Fool watched as the people faded like phantoms, to disappear for ever back into the stream of time. In the deep silent space within him, he beheld the most beautiful sight he had ever seen. Almost blinded by its radiance, he perceived that it was the energetic reality of himself. No longer shrouded in material flesh and bone, he was a golden being in the divine mind of God.

⌒✦⌒

XX

JUDGEMENT / LE JUGEMENT

SYMBOLISM

The Fool has awakened from the dream to realise the awful truth of existence: that the world and all its sordidness, violence and injustice is his self. Yet all is seen to be perfect in an unalterable state of equilibrium, with the knowledge that there is nothing to prove or to change, and that everything has served in his spiritual quest. Through the gradual realisation of his own authenticity, the Fool has transcended the need to be reborn on the endless Wheel of Fortune.

In the Tarot card, three figures behold a winged celestial being. The central figure is the Fool in his physical earthly guise. The winged herald is his spiritual reality, the divine essence behind the inner sun, now appearing as the radiant vision of the creative idea of all he has ever been. The other figures, the man and the woman, represent the totality of the Fool's earthly experience. Through the living and dying process, the lessons of life in all its rich diversity have contributed to a profound understanding of the human condition. The Fool has been resurrected from the tomb of ignorance through the integrity of life and the refusal to compromise with the falsity of his self. Now alive as never before, he summons humanity with a blast of his horn for all who can hear and receive the good news.

Man's greatest fear is what others may think or say about him. On the outside he may appear immune to criticism, but within he is often afflicted with self-judgement, the most subtle and insidious emotion of all. From this arises the judgement of others and the inability to accept life as it is. To compensate for the separation from love and the fear to trust his own integrity, man invented a conscience. This psychological prop enabled him to reflect on his actions and those of others — and then to judge them. Morally bound to the notions of good and bad, and right and wrong, he is now frequently held to ransom, manipulated by the double standards and hypocrisy of the world.

Only in the surrender of self-judgement can true creativity be expressed. In giving up the terrible strain of supporting the false in existence, the Fool has emerged as a realised being on earth. Through the love of truth and the dissolution of his negative emotions, the real

Magician, with his purified wand, is now able to truly love, knowing that his only purpose in existence is to bring woman back to life.

DIVINING JUDGEMENT

The essence of Judgement is self-knowledge, enabling a new quality to reveal itself to awaken the individual to his true purpose of life.

As an OPENING card, Judgement can symbolise a new depth of comprehension, giving an original insight into a situation. It indicates the emergence of a new quality through the surrender of past concepts. There may be the opportunity to implement a new idea, or to take action which may contribute to a profound change in one's life.

As a card in ASSISTANCE, Judgement signifies a deep self-knowledge that enables an individual to perceive the integrity of a situation. The refinement of all that has been as the experience of living can now be utilised in an ease of communication and an absence of trying.

In OPPOSITION, recurring waves of self-doubt and insecurity, through the judgement of oneself, may result in a depletion of energy. There can be a fear of rejection and judgement of others, and emotional pressure to conform to the old patterns and influences of the past.

As the OUTCOME, Judgement symbolises the realisation of the rightness and joyousness of pure creativity. There is the ability to impart one's knowledge with a uniqueness and authority that has arisen from the virtue of one's experience of life.

❄

THE WORLD

The Myth of the World

In a state of loving communion with the earth, the Fool held in deep respect and gratitude the essence of mother. Her selfless love in bearing the pain of childbirth, and devotion to the needs of her children, replicated the giving of the one Earth Mother in her abundant nature.

The Fool, having realised his purpose as the true Magician, loved woman with the purity of his being. Descending deeper into her ground of love, he was now able to bring into existence her timeless beauty. The seed of the Empress, sown so long ago, had come to fruition; in the recognition of his noble purpose, he had received the authority of the Emperor through her finest feminine energies. By entering the furnace of love, he had reached the High Priestess, discovering her mystery in the sensuality of woman. As the divine Charioteer, he could now release the reins of his charges, so obedient were they to their master.

The justice of life was such that all he had sacrificed through the hardships endured were now returning to him, not in conflict and division, but through the harmonious integrity of life. In his devotion to love and truth, all had been done.

The Fool now received the garland of the pure of heart, as the Spirit of the Earth embraced the child who had left the womb of life so long ago. In a place of extraordinary stillness and grace, he beheld the glory behind everything on earth, the one transcendent being that was God. Resonating with the oneness of universal life, he realised in that eternal moment the Lord, the container of all knowledge; yet holding on to nothing, he was pastless and liberated from time.

XXI

THE WORLD / LE MONDE

SYMBOLISM

The Fool has returned to the earth. It is the summation of an epic journey and the return to innocence. In this state of vulnerability to love, he is aligned with the great will of life, whose external forces no longer threaten and oppose but combine to serve his destiny.

In the Tarot card, a naked figure is pictured within an oval wreath. It is the symbol of androgynous Man in the original state of unity between the male and female principles. A veil covering the genitals conceals life's great secret: the mystery of the procreative part or godhead. The unusual posture of the left leg bent behind the right knee, which was seen in the Emperor and Hangman, is a symbol of stability and alignment with the harmony of the universe. The laurel wreath is the symbol of spiritual attainment; it is the prize won through courage, heroism and valour, and the end of the need to be anything other than at one with the whole. Appearing in the upper and lower corners of the card are an angel, eagle, lion and ox, symbolising the elements as the outer reflection of man's true nature.

Man's world mirrors the ignorance and hopelessness of existence. While there is faith in what it seems to offer, there will be no incentive to turn inwards to begin the journey back. Man is limited only by his lack of vision and the false identification with his self, which attaches him to re-experience the emotional pain of existence. The personal sacrifice in taking responsibility for life as an ordinary man or woman conflicts with the world's idea of liberation. The Fool is a revolutionary, a freedom fighter so passionately inspired by the love of the unknown that in changing himself within, he has changed his world without through the virtue of his life.

The earth is all that is natural in creation. The world is man-made, humanity's need to impose itself on the order of things. Living in an aura outside himself, man has erected a mental barrier of thought and information around the simplicity of his being. With his focus on the external world, he has left the joyousness and sensual delight of his body. Yet something, no matter how far he loses himself in his world, will not let him rest for long: this is the calling of love, the missing part of himself that compels him to forever search in existence until he finds it.

DIVINING THE WORLD

The World is the synthesis of the Tarot. It can be a mirror of true character, reflecting an individual's honesty to life and his part in the great body of humanity.

As an OPENING card, the World can symbolise the knowledge of the impersonal nature of love, and enormous potential to break with any compromise that is suppressing the joy of life. Although there is a great perception of the integrity of the whole, there can be an idealistic vision, making the questioner distanced from the practicalities of the world.

As a card in ASSISTANCE, the World signifies an expanded vision, enabling the questioner to perceive a greater depth of reality in a situation. There is the potential for past fragments of unresolved circumstances to merge into a harmonious solution.

In OPPOSITION, it may be necessary to stand alone, as the support of others may be withdrawn. However, caution is advised against taking a unilateral stance if there is a tendency towards personal aggrandisement.

As an OUTCOME, the World can symbolise the natural completion of a phase or cycle. There can be a sense of fulfilment in the realisation that what has been achieved has contributed in some way to the whole. It can represent the severing of the umbilical cord, whereby an individual soars into a new phase of life with the freedom to move in any direction.

❅

All things in creation now served the Fool, who returned to the world as the Lord of his kingdom.

The journey was over, yet life was never-ending. As long as it were necessary, he would remain in existence to impart the sublime knowledge he had realised: that the purpose of life was to delight in the joy and beauty of the earth in the sacred love between man and woman.